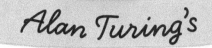
Alan Turing's

Logic Puzzles
For Kids

This edition published in 2023 by Arcturus Publishing Limited
26/27 Bickels Yard, 151–153 Bermondsey Street,
London SE1 3HA

Author: Eric Saunders
Illustrator: Eve O'Brien
Illustrations on the following pages are from Shutterstock: 33, 38, 46, 67, 73, 93, 98.
Editor: Lydia Halliday
Design Manager: Jessica Holliland
Managing Editor: Joe Harris

CH010499NT
Supplier 10, Date 0723, PI0004110

Printed in the UK

Letter Cubes

Here are three different views of the same cube. Which letters appear on the faces that are opposite the ones with the letters A, D, and E?

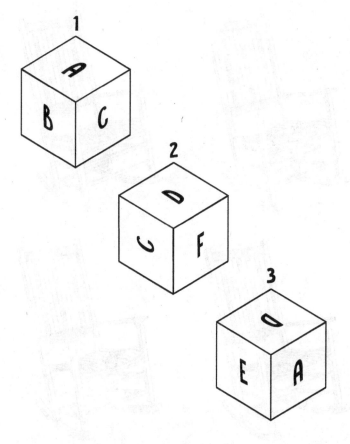

Spot the Difference

In each of the pictures below, there is one detail different from the other pictures. Can you spot the one difference in every case?

Matching Pairs

Sort these squares into matching pairs!

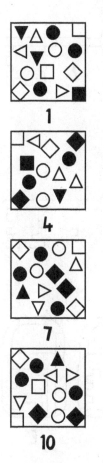

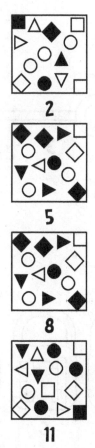

1 **2** **3**

4 **5** **6**

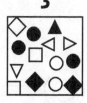

7 **8** **9**

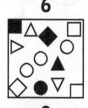

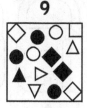

10 **11** **12**

Locks

Which key fits each lock?

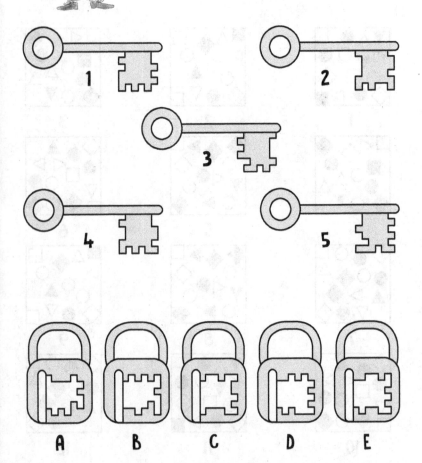

From Head to Hoof

Find a way through this zebra maze, from the head at the top to the hoof at the bottom.

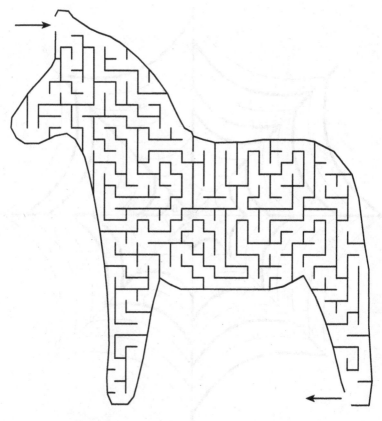

The Way Home

Bella the spider is in the middle of her web and needs to get back to her home, which is in a little hole at the bottom of the web. Which one of the three routes should she take?

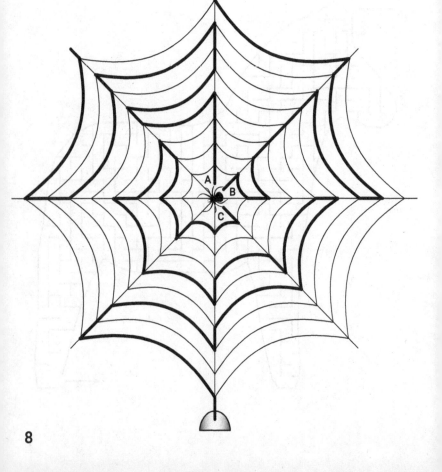

Reflections

Butterfly B is a horizontal reflection of butterfly A. Which of the alternatives (D, E, F, or G) is a horizontal reflection of butterfly C?

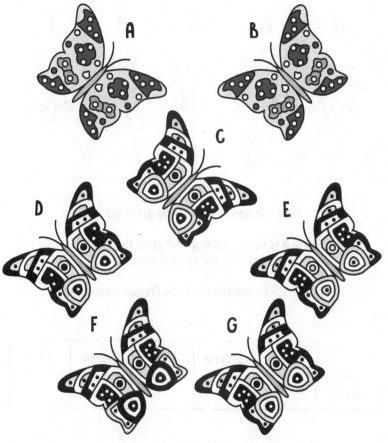

Fairy Magic

Fairy Freya has a magic spell that uses five different wands! She waves each, one by one, over her friend Fred the Frog to turn him into a handsome prince. You can perform the magical spell, too, if you can figure out the order in which Freya uses her five wands.

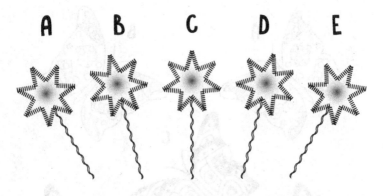

Wand C is used immediately after wand B.

Wand A is used earlier in the spell than wand D, but later in the spell than wand E.

Wand E isn't used first in Fairy Freya's magic spell.

	First	Second	Third	Fourth	Fifth
Wand					

Beach balls

Only two of these beach balls are identical in every way. Can you find them?

1

2

3

4

5

6

7

8

9

Find the Buttons

Can you find three buttons that are identical in every way?

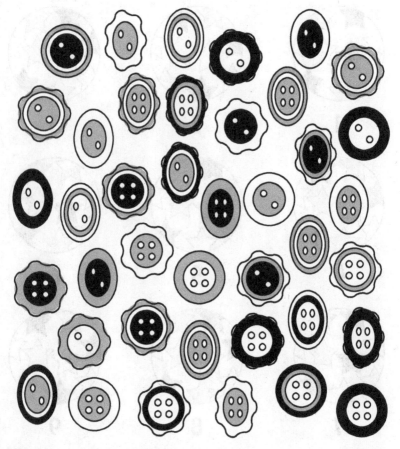

Sequences

Follow both of these sequences starting from the circle at the top. What should be in the central circle of each diagram?

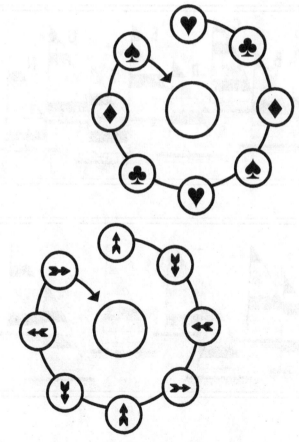

Yacht Racing

Kate took two photos of a yacht race. The bottom one was taken ten minutes after the top one. In that time, the yachts had changed position, and one had dropped out of the race. Which one is not in the second picture?

Building Blocks

Which of these brick towers has been constructed with the largest number of bricks?

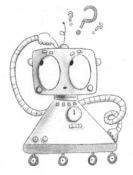

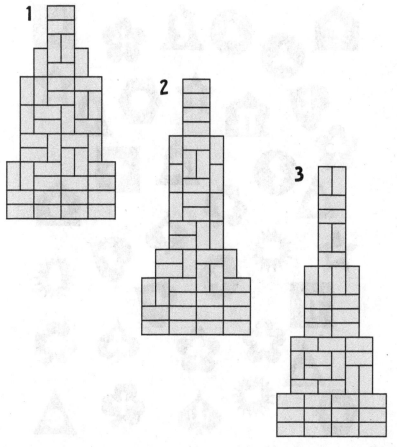

Matching Pair

Each black shape has another shape cut out of it. Can you find two black shapes that match exactly?

Patterns

Fill in the two empty boxes with the missing parts of the pattern in each of these four designs.

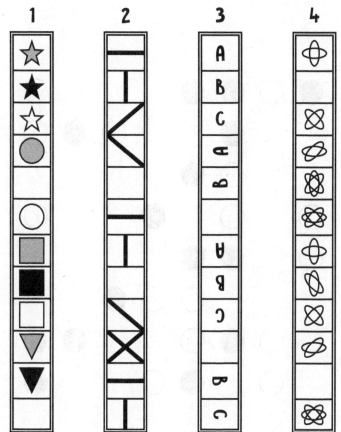

Connections

Connect one white circle to one black circle each time, using either a horizontal or vertical line. No line may cross any other line or pass through any circle. One line is already in place.

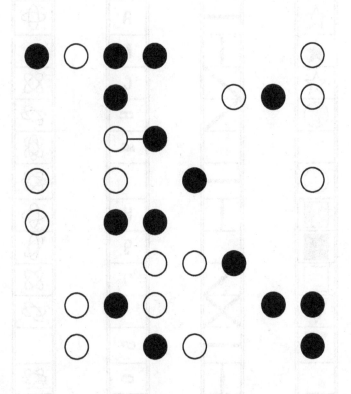

Symbolism

Each of these squares should contain one or two symbols from the numbered square to the left of its horizontal row, plus one or two symbols from the lettered square above its vertical column. However, one square doesn't follow this rule. Which is the odd one out?

Mirror Image

Only one kite is an exact mirror image of the one at the top left. Which?

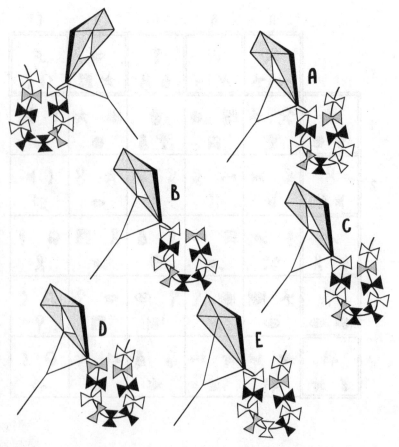

★☆☆

Hidden Treasure

Jayden has arrived on Treasure Island. He is looking for a pirate's treasure hidden in a chest buried in the ground, and he has a map. Help him find the treasure chest by following the instructions below. For example, 1W means that you should move one square west, 2N means that you should move two squares north, and so on. Start in the square marked with a star, and place a cross in the square where the treasure chest is buried.

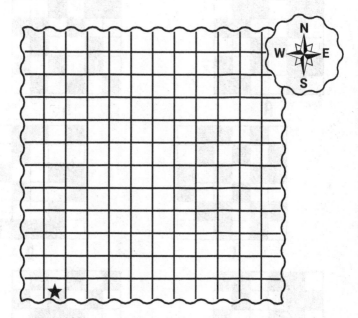

1W, 2N, 4E, 5N, 2W, 3S, 4E, 3S, 4E,
5N, 2W, 1N, 2W, 4N, 5W, 3S, 3E, 1N,
5E, 6S, 1W

21

Odd One Out

One of these is different to the others in some way. Can you discover which is the odd one out, and say why?

A

B

C

D

E

F

Wedges

Which wedge has been removed:
A, B, C, or D?

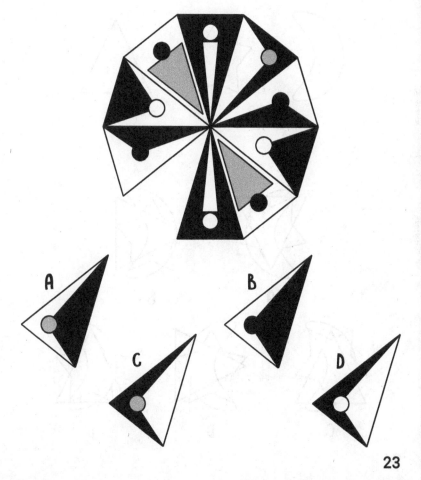

Overlaps

If the three designs at the top are made to overlap without reflecting or rotating any, which design would appear: A, B, C, D, or E?

A

B

C

D

E

Black and White

Shade in the squares on the right-hand side of the grid to complete a symmetrical, mirror image pattern.

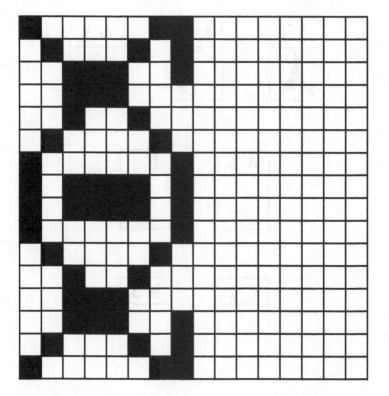

Shapes and Shades

Look at the pictures below. Each has a letter and a number above it. The letter stands for the shape, and the number indicates the shading of that shape. Draw and shade a shape into each empty box, so that it matches the code above it.

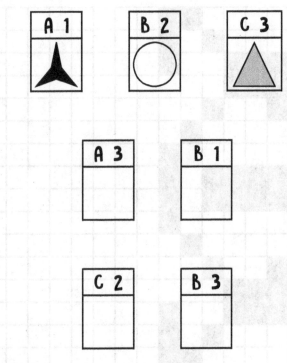

Shapes and Symbols

Which of these three shapes can be used four times to divide up the grid, so that each area contains exactly seven different symbols? Any shape can be rotated or flipped over.

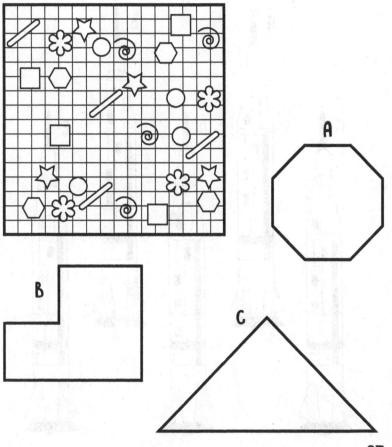

A

B

C

Spot the Difference

In each of the pictures below, there is one detail different from the other pictures. Can you spot the one difference in every picture?

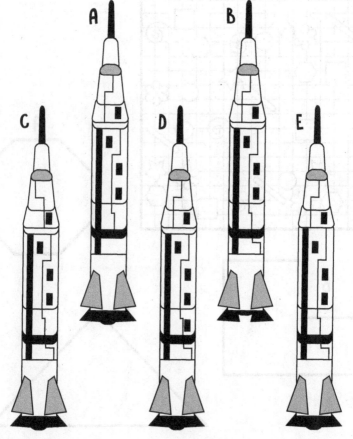

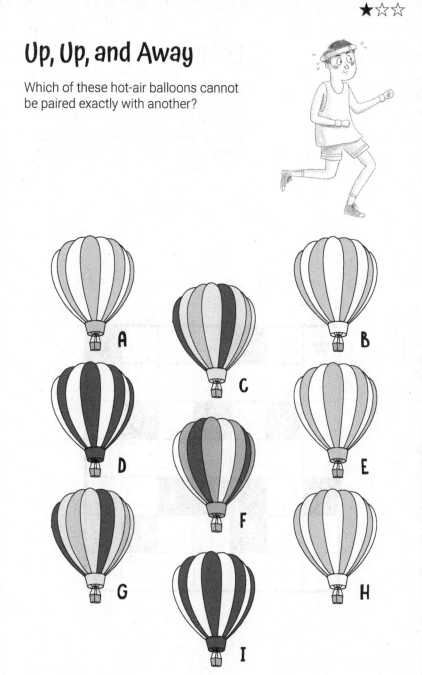

Up, Up, and Away

Which of these hot-air balloons cannot be paired exactly with another?

Loopy

Starting at the star in the top left square, draw a line that passes through every white square once only and ends up back at the star in the top left square. Do not pass through any black squares.

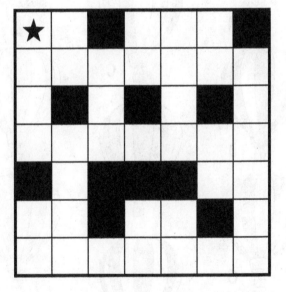

Filling In

Which black shape will exactly fill the hole in the large black shape? None may be rotated, reflected, or flipped over.

A

B

C

D

E

F

★☆☆

Big Black Ant

Which silhouette matches that of the big black ant shown here?

Parasol Pairs

Can you group these 14 parasols into seven matching pairs?

Shape Shading

Shade in all of the shapes that are triangles to reveal the hidden picture.

Matching Pairs

Can you pair up each gift box with a letter to its twin that has a number?

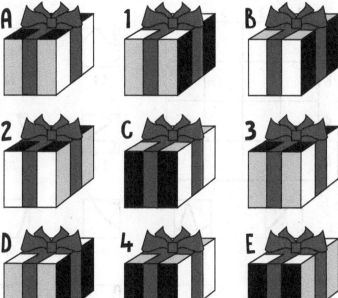

Mystery Picture

Copy the contents of each square into the empty grid, using the grid references below each piece, in order to reveal the mystery picture!

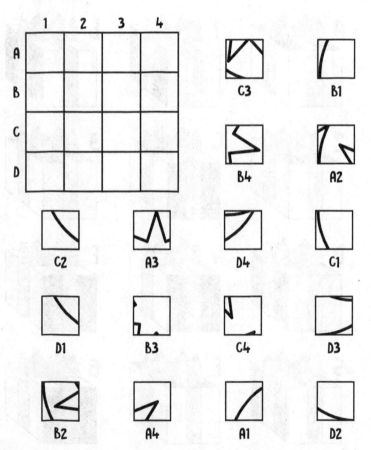

Matching Mugs

Can you find three mugs that are exactly the same?

Ball Game

Find a way through this grid, from top left to bottom right, only stepping on the balls in this order:

You can move up, down, left, and right, but not diagonally.

Futoshiki

Fill the grid so that every horizontal row
and vertical column contains all the
numbers 1 to 6.

Any arrow (>) in the grid always points
toward a square that contains a
lower number.

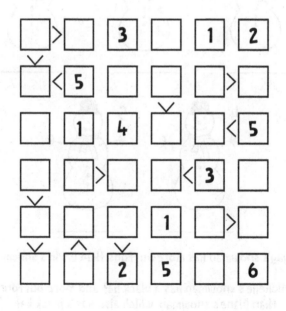

Snowmen

Can you discover who built each of these five snowmen? Write the name of its builder on the line beneath each snowman.

Sanjay's snowman has more buttons than David's snowman.

Michelle's snowman has a black hat and more buttons than Diane's snowman, which also has a black hat.

Luke's snowman has a white hat.

David's snowman has a higher number than Diane's snowman.

Battleships

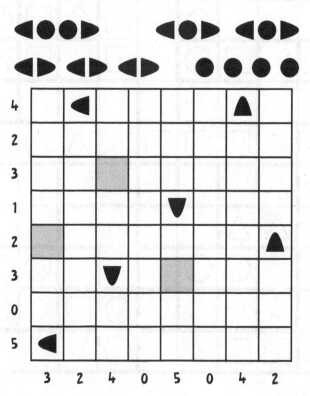

There are 10 battleships in this grid: one ship filling four squares, two ships filling three squares, three filling two squares, and four filling one square, as below. The ships go across or down, but not diagonally. The numbers on the sides of the grid show how many squares in each row and column contain part of a ship. Some parts of ships have been placed in the grid. Shaded squares indicate the sea. The battleships must not touch each other across, down, or diagonally. Can you figure out where they all go?

Shape Sets

Draw shapes into each square, so that no two areas that touch (even at a corner) share the same shape. Squares in every heavily outlined set should contain the same shape, as with the examples shown. The shapes to be used are shown above the grid.

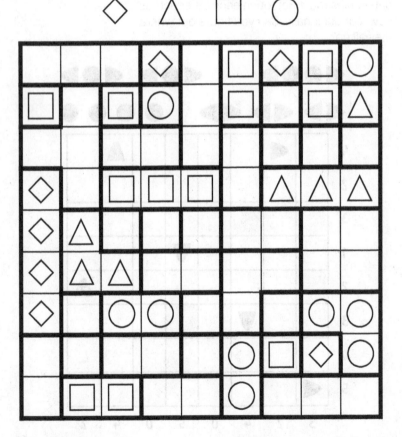

★★☆

Easy as A, B, C?

Fill in the letters in this grid. Each row and column in the grid should have the letters A, B, C, and D, plus a black square that appears just once. Letters and numbers around the outside indicate where you come across this letter when looking from that side. For example, in the middle row, D3 means that D is the third letter that can be seen when looking from that side. Two black squares and one letter have been given.

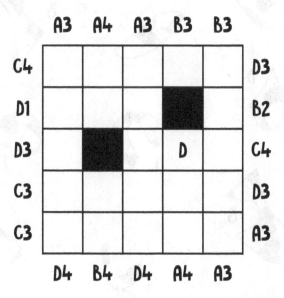

	A3	A4	A3	B3	B3	
C4						D3
D1				■		B2
D3		■		D		C4
C3						D3
C3						A3
	D4	B4	D4	A4	A3	

43

★★☆

Broken-Hearted

Four hearts have each been broken into three pieces. Can you match the pieces of every heart? Any piece can be rotated.

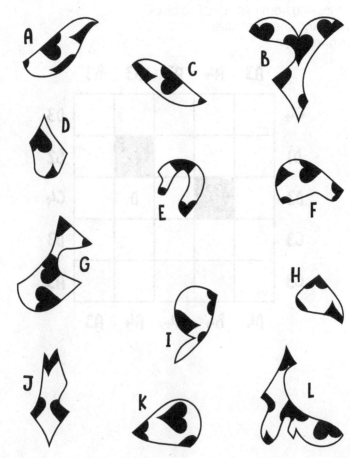

A

Crowning Glory

King Khaled, Queen Cora, Prince Paul, and Princess Pilar each wear crowns studded with white diamonds and black pearls. Use the clues to find out which crown belongs to each.

King Khaled's crown has three fewer pearls than Queen Cora's crown.

Princess Pilar's crown has three more pearls than Prince Paul's crown.

Prince Paul's crown has fewer diamonds than King Khaled's crown.

Crown 1

_____

Crown 2

_____

Crown 3

_____

Crown 4

_____

Matching Jackets

Each of these jackets can be paired with another, identical jacket. Which one has no exact match?

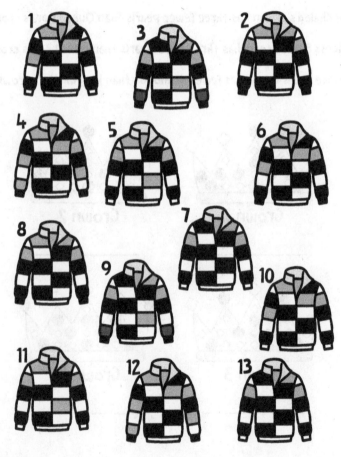

Blowing Bubbles

Count the number of bubbles that are floating in the air to find out how many Mario blew.

Lucy blew two more bubbles than Mark.

Stella blew six fewer bubbles than Mark.

Mark blew ten bubbles.

Mario blew all of the other bubbles!

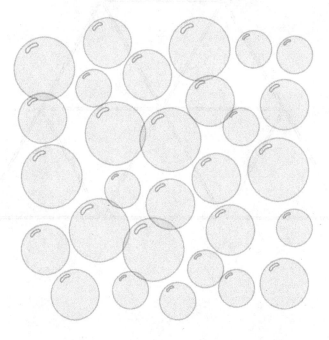

Triangle Challenge

Remove three lines, so you are left with nine triangles.

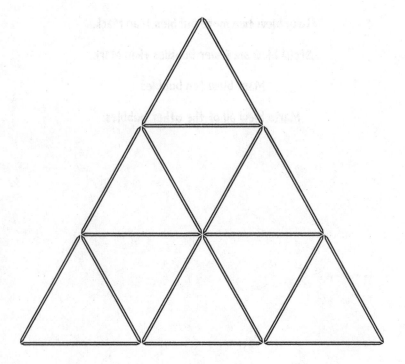

Water Buckets

When the water is turned on, it will pour into the top tank. Which bucket will fill up first?

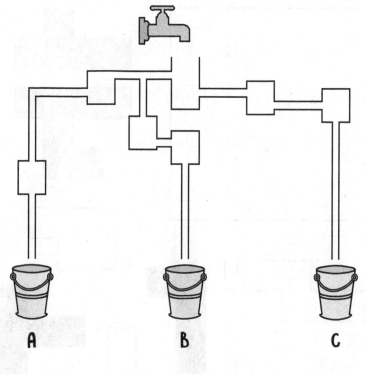

A   B   C

Square Shape

Can you fit all of these pieces into the square, so that it is completely filled, with no overhanging or overlapping shapes? No piece may be rotated or flipped over.

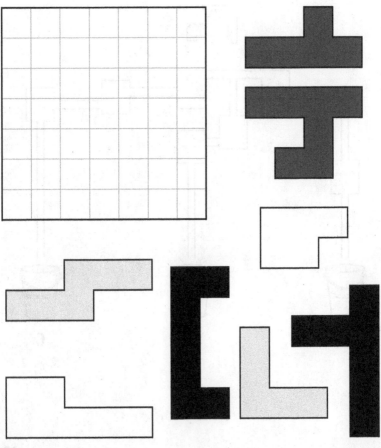

Wall Reflection

Nicky built a wall using three different shades of bricks. It rained several days later, and the wall is now reflected in a puddle. Can you finish shading in the design in the puddle and complete the reflection?

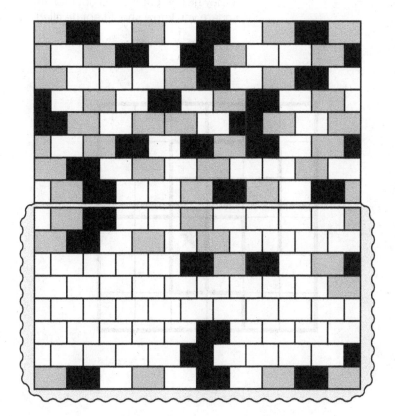

★★☆

Star Shine

Every row and column of this grid should contain just one star. Squares in every heavily outlined set should also contain just one star, as with the example shown. Stars cannot be placed in any square that touches a square containing another star, either at a side or at a corner. When solving, it may help to put a small dot into any square you know should not be filled.

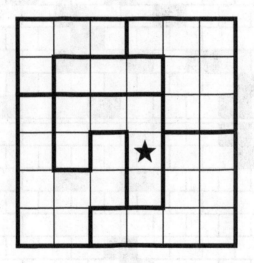

Tic-Tac-Toe

Place either O or X in each empty square, so that no four consecutive squares in a straight line in any direction (horizontally, vertically, or diagonally) contain more than three of the same symbol.

	O	O	O		X			X
		O	X		X	X		
	O				X	X		O
		X	X	X				O
	O				O	O	X	
O						O	O	
X	O		X		O			
O	O	X	X		X			X
	X			X	X		O	X

Dot-to-Dot

Connect all the dots in the grid to form one continuous, looping line. Only use horizontal and vertical lines between dots, not diagonals. You can only use each dot once, and you cannot cross a line that's already been drawn. Some lines are in place to get you started.

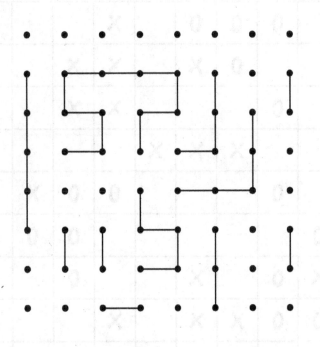

Mouse Maze

Can you help this mouse reach her lunch by going through the maze from the top to the bottom?

Star Turn

Starting with the star in the top left square, draw a line that passes through every white square once only and ends up back at the star in the top left square. Do not pass through any black squares.

Sun, Moon, and Star

Divide this grid into areas of three squares each, in such a way that each area contains one sun, one moon, and one star. One area is already shown.

Cheerful Chimp

Which silhouette exactly matches that of this adorable little chimp?

Treasure Hunt

The hunt is on for Pirate Pete's hidden chest of gold coins! Nell has a map and directions, so can you help her locate the treasure? Start at the arrow, and follow the clues at the bottom of the page, then place an X to show her where to start digging.

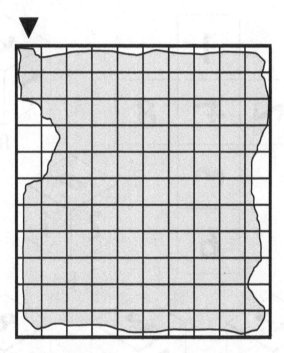

N
↑
W ←——|——→ E
↓
S

2S, 2E, 3S, 1E, 2S, 2W, 1S, 2E, 1S, 2W,

1S, 4E, 3N, 1W, 1N, 2E, 3S, 2E, 2N, 1W,

3N, 1E, 1N, 2W, 1S, 3W, 1N, 1E, 1N, 1E

★★☆

Box Clever

When this shape is folded to form a cube, just one of the five options (A, B, C, D, or E) can be produced. Which is it?

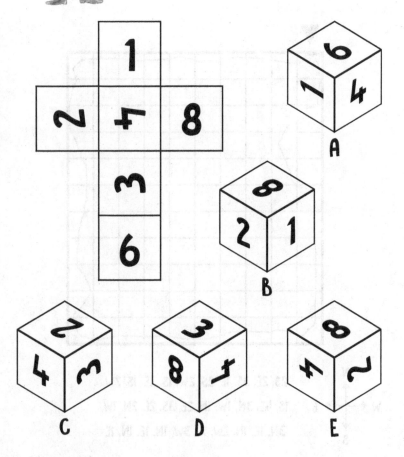

Viking Ships

Pair the identical Viking ships. One in each pair is going in the opposite direction to the other. Which one cannot be paired?

A Perfect Fit

When rotated, which two of these pieces will fit exactly into the holes in the circle below?

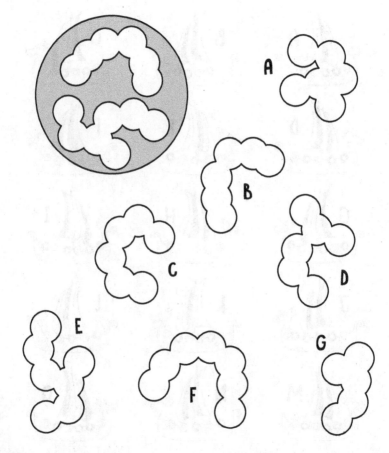

A

B

C

D

E

F

G

Birthday Boys

Six children have birthdays in different months from January to June. Can you find out when each child celebrates their birthday?

Jacob's birthday is later in the year than Lola's, but it's two months earlier than Oscar's birthday.

Ethan's birthday is earlier in the year than Michael's, but it's two months later than Olivia's birthday.

Olivia's birthday is the month after Lola's birthday.

Month	Child
January	
February	
March	
April	
May	
June	

Whose House?

Five friends live in the houses you see below. Follow the clues to discover who lives in each house.

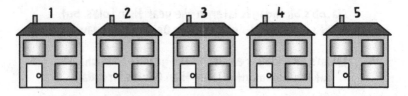

Oliver's house number is higher than Jake's.

Ava's house number is lower than Lucas's, and Lucas's house number is lower than Amelia's.

Oliver's house number is lower than Ava's.

	House 1	House 2	House 3	House 4	House 5
Lucas					
Amelia					
Jake					
Ava					
Oliver					

Building Blocks

Which of these piles contains the most building blocks? Apart from those on the bottom layer, every building block sits on top of one other, so no block is floating in midair.

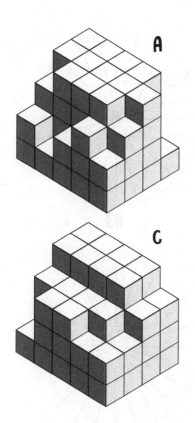

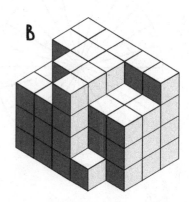

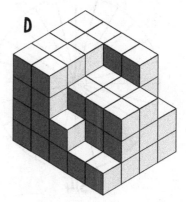

Pieces of Pie

Shade in the areas shown beneath each pie chart.

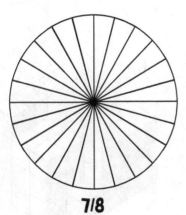

7/8

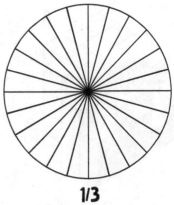

1/3

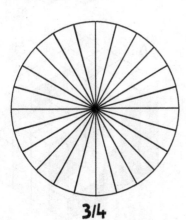

3/4

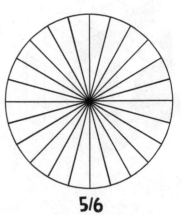

5/6

Robotics

Which three of these parts are not needed to build the main robot?

1

2

3

4

5

6

7

8

9

10

11

12

13

Square Challenge

Remove two lines to leave just six squares. Can you find two different ways of doing this?

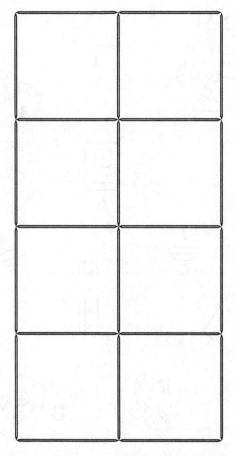

Moon Gazing

Every row and column of this grid should contain just one moon. Squares in every heavily outlined set should also contain just one moon, as with the example shown. Moons cannot be placed in any square that touches a square containing another moon, either at a side or at a corner. When solving, it may help to put a small dot into any square you know should not be filled.

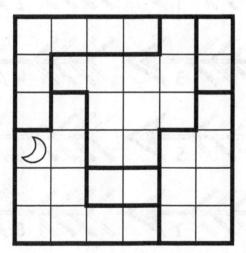

A Matching Pair

Which two arrows are identical?

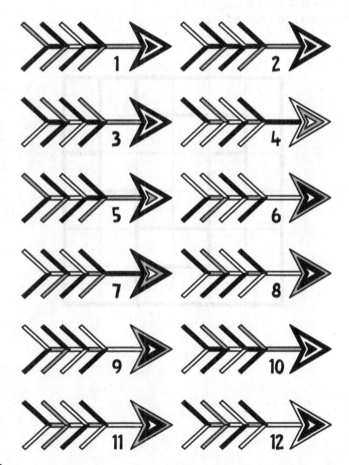

Mystery Picture

★★☆

Copy the contents of each square into the empty grid using the grid references below each piece, in order to reveal the mystery picture!

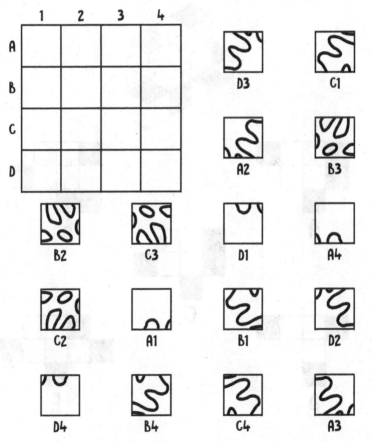

A Bird's-Eye View

Imagine looking down from above at these building blocks. Which view (A, B, C, D, or E) matches the top down view of the cubes?

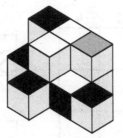

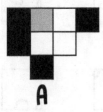

A

B

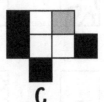

C

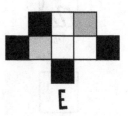

D

E

One Piece Missing

Which piece of the jigsaw puzzle is missing from the scattered pieces? Identify it by its column letter and row number.

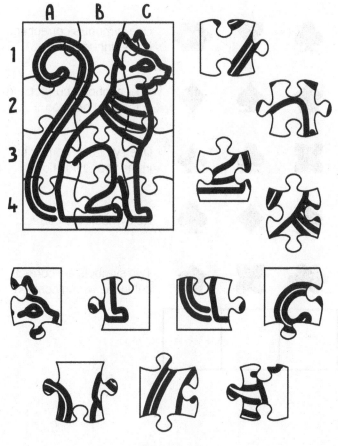

Crack the Code

Can you discover the correct code by reading and comparing the clues next to each incorrect combination? The correct code is made up of three different symbols.

One symbol is correct and in the right position.

One symbol is correct and in the right position.

One symbol is correct but in the wrong position.

No symbols are correct.

Two symbols are correct but in the wrong position.

Circle Game

Some of the circles in this puzzle are already black. Fill in more white circles, so that the number of black circles totals the number inside the area they surround. The black circles should be next to each other.

When solving, it may help to put a small dot into any circle that you know should not be filled.

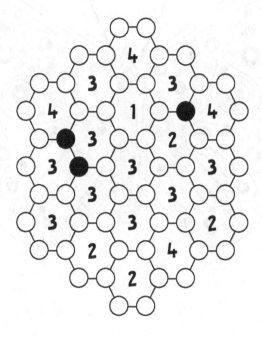

Spot the Difference

The wings of this butterfly should be a mirror image of one another, but there are six differences. Can you spot them all?

Combiku

Each horizontal row and vertical column should contain four different shapes and four different numbers. Every square will contain a number and a shape, and no combination may be repeated anywhere else in the puzzle; so, for instance, if a square contains a triangle with a 3 inside, then no other square can contain a triangle with a 3 inside. Some numbers and shapes are already in place to start you off.

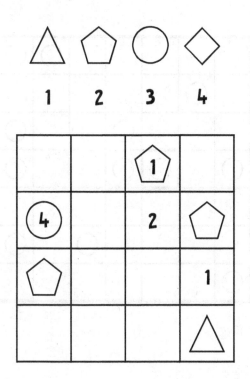

Squaring the Circles

Divide this grid into areas of either 1x1, 2x2, or 3x3 smaller squares, so that each area contains just one circle. One has already been done to get you off to a good start.

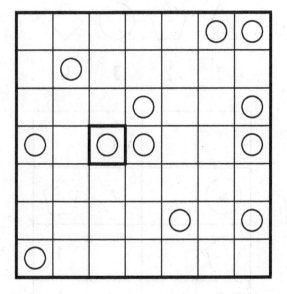

Consecutive Sudoku

Fill the empty squares in this grid, so that every horizontal row, vertical column, and mini grid contain different numbers between 1 and 6. Wherever two touching squares contain consecutive numbers, there is a bar between them. Consecutive numbers have a difference of one: For example, the numbers 1 and 2 are consecutive, but 1 and 3 are not.

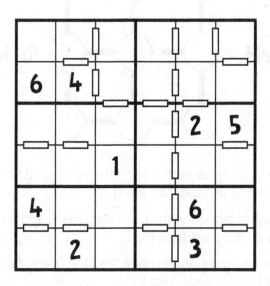

Letter Locator

Every circle should contain a different letter of the alphabet from A to I. Use the clues to discover their locations.

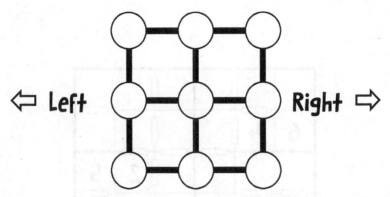

⇦ Left   Right ⇨

1 The A is higher on the page than the I, and farther right on the page than the H.

2 The B is higher on the page than the E, and farther left on the page than the G.

3 The F is lower on the page than the D, and farther right on the page than the C.

4 The G is farther left on the page than the F, and higher on the page than the C.

5 The H is farther right on the page than the I, and higher on the page than the A.

Six Shapes

Every square in the grid below should contain one each of the six shapes shown, with none appearing more than once in any row or column.

Shapes on the outside of some rows and columns show which shape will appear first when looking from that direction. Can you complete the grid by filling all of the empty squares?

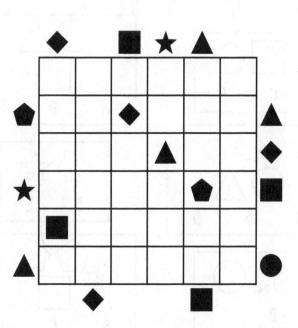

Shape Selection

Each letter represents a shape. Look at the letters in each box of shapes, and compare them to the letters and shapes in other boxes. Which shapes are represented by the letters A and E? Draw them in the empty box below.

A   E

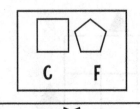

C   F

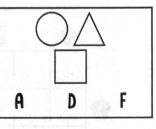

A   D   F

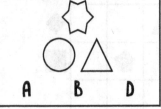

A   B   D

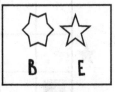

B   E

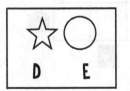

D   E

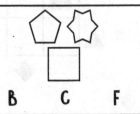

B   C   F

Shape Sorting

Place one of the symbols below the grid into each empty square, so that no horizontal row, vertical column, or diagonal line of either two, three, or four squares contains the same symbol.

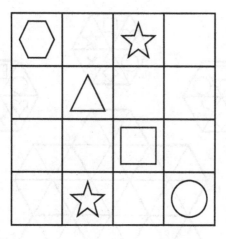

Hexagony

Can you place the hexagons into the grid, so that where any hexagon touches another along a straight line, the contents of both triangles is the same? No rotation of any hexagon is allowed!

Shape Sequence

What comes next in this sequence of shapes? Choose one answer from A, B, C, or D. Clue: Look at the number of sides of each shape.

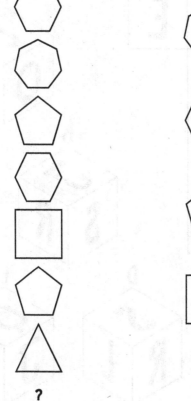

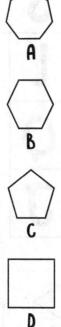

Cube Folding

When this T shape is folded into a cube, which one of the following will it look like: A, B, C, D, or E?

Connections

Connect one white circle to one black circle each time, using either a horizontal or vertical line. No line may cross any other line or pass through any circle.

Numberlink

Travel from circle to circle in any direction along the lines to find the sequence 1-2-3-4-5-6-7, which appears once only.

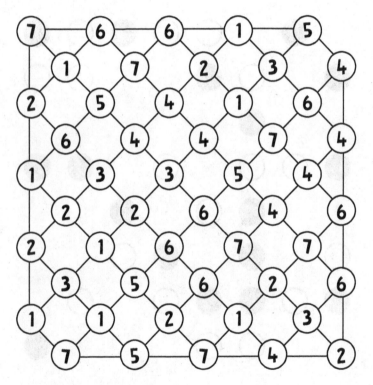

Dotted Division

Divide this grid into areas of either 1x1, 2x2, or 3x3 smaller squares, so that each area contains just one dot. One has already been done to get you off to a good start.

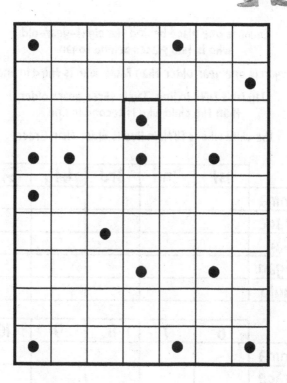

Ice-Cream Cones

Five children want to buy ice-cream cones, and are patiently waiting to be served. What position is each child in the line, and how old is he or she?

Emma is one place behind the eight-year-old, who is two places behind Logan.

Logan is one year older than Paulo, who is third in line.

Jay isn't fifth in line. Jay is three years older than the child who is second in line.

The child who is fifth in line is older than Grace.

	1st	2nd	3rd	4th	5th
Emma					
Grace					
Jay					
Logan					
Paulo					

	6	7	8	9	10
Emma					
Grace					
Jay					
Logan					
Paulo					

Crack the Code

Can you figure out the correct code by reading and comparing the clues next to each incorrect combination? The correct code is made up of four different numbers.

2	5	6	1	Three numbers are correct but in the wrong position.
1	7	2	3	One number is correct and in the right position.
1	8	7	6	Two numbers are correct but in the wrong position.
8	7	2	4	Two numbers are correct and in the right position.

Dot-to-Dot

Connect all the dots in the grid to form one continuous looping line. Only use horizontal and vertical lines between dots, not diagonals. You can only use each dot once, and you cannot cross a line that's already been drawn. Some lines are in place to get you started.

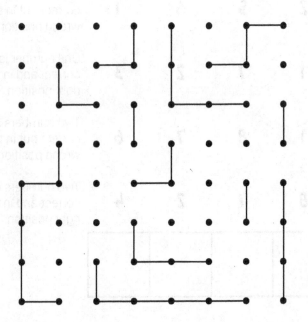

Robot Assembly

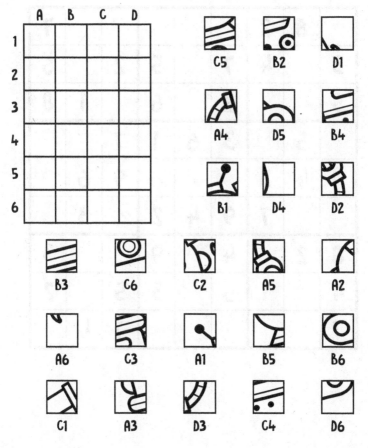

Copy the contents of each square into the empty grid, using the grid references below each piece, in order to make your very own robot!

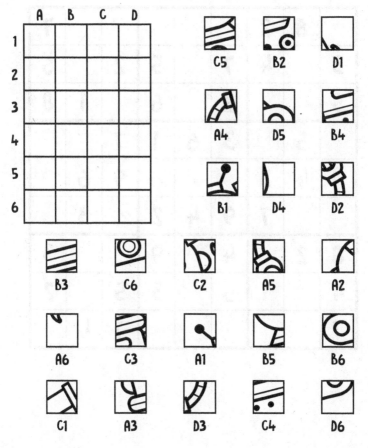

Sudoku

Fill the empty squares in the grid, so that there is one of every number from 1 to 9 in each row, column, and mini grid of nine squares.

★★★

	8	2						7
3		4	7		5	2		6
5			2		6		1	8
	5		3	6	1	7		
	4	3				9	6	
		7	9	4	2		3	
8	2		4		9			3
4		1	6		3	5		2
7						1	4	

Star Shine

Every row and column of this grid should contain just one star. Squares in every heavily outlined set should also contain just one star, as with the example shown. Stars cannot be placed in any square that touches a square containing another star, either at a side or at a corner. When solving, it may help to put a small dot in any square you know should not be filled.

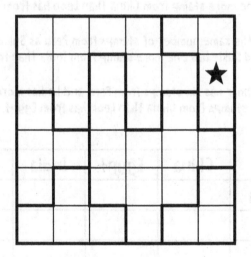

Stamp Collections

Four children are about to add to their stamp collections, with various numbers of stamps from different countries.

Every child has four different quantities (either 6, 7, 8, or 9) of stamps from each country, and no two or more children have exactly the same number of stamps from the same country. Can you discover how many stamps every child has from each of the four countries?

Maria has two more stamps from India than from Peru, and she has one more stamp from China than Leon has from China.

Leon has the same number of stamps from Peru as Sukie has from Egypt, and Sukie has one more stamp from India than from China.

Omar has six stamps from Peru and he has more stamps from China than Leon has from Egypt.

	China	Egypt	India	Peru
Maria				
Leon				
Omar				
Sukie				

Shady

Shade in some of the empty squares, so that when added together the total number of black squares in a row and column is equal to the number in that row, plus the number in that column. The bottom row and far right column have already been fully completed. It may help to put a small dot in those squares that you know cannot be black.

2				
1		3		■
	4			■
			4	
	■			3

Turtle Teaser

Each of these five turtles has a different name, and each is a different age: either 2, 3, 4, 5, or 6 years old. Use the clues to correctly identify each turtle and its age.

Terry is two years older than turtle A, who isn't Tina.

Turtle B is four years old.

Turtle B is younger than Thomas (who is turtle C).

Timmy is one year older than Tina, who is two.

Tara is turtle B and is older than turtle D.

	Turtle	Age
Tara		
Terry		
Thomas		
Timmy		
Tina		

Weighty Matters

Which shape is heaviest, and which is lightest? All identical shapes weigh the same.

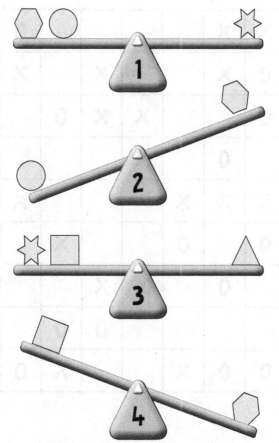

★★★

Tic-Tac-Toe

Place either O or X into each empty square, so that no four consecutive squares in a straight line in any direction (horizontally, vertically, or diagonally) contain more than three of the same symbol.

	X	X					O	X
X	O	X			X		X	O
X	O			X	X	O		O
O		O		X				
	X	X	X				X	
	O		O			X		X
		O		X	X			X
					O	O		
X	O	O	X			X	O	O

The Wrong Labels

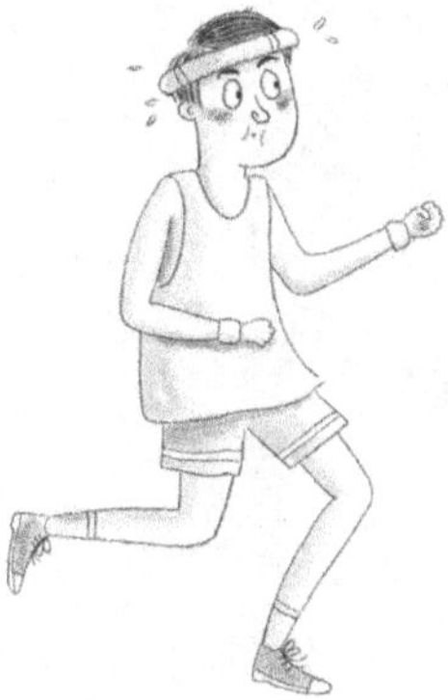

Here are three large boxes. One contains hats, another contains scarves, and another contains gloves. However, the box marked "Hats" doesn't have any hats in it, the one marked "Scarves" doesn't have any scarves in it, and the one marked "Gloves" doesn't have any gloves in it. In other words, they are all in the wrong boxes.

If you take a scarf out of the box on the top, what items are in the other two boxes?

If you take a glove out of the box on the top, what items are in the other two boxes?

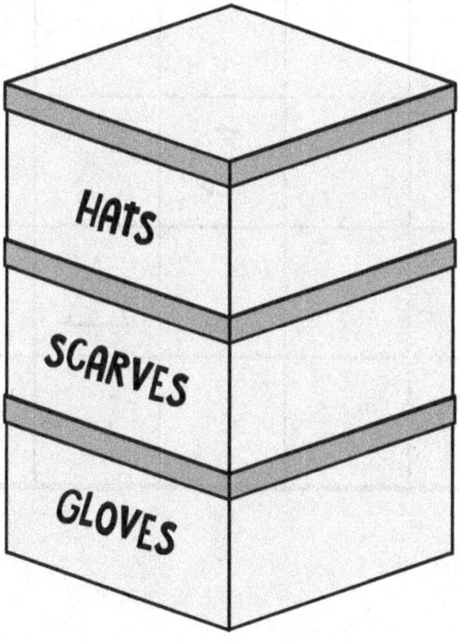

Square Shapes

Each square in the grid below should be filled with one of five different shapes. In every row, column, and long diagonal line, there are five different shapes. Some are already in place. Can you fill the empty squares?

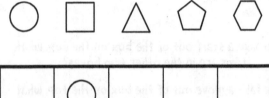

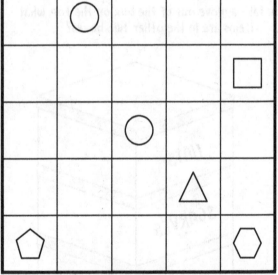

Islands

Shade in some more of the squares in the grid below, so that each number is inside either a square or rectangular island made up of exactly that number of squares. No islands can share an edge, although any may touch at a corner. The shaded squares that surround the islands cannot be 2x2 or larger.

1					2		
	■	4		■			2
					6		
	6					■	3
				■			
8					4		

School Subjects

Each child in this puzzle likes a different subject at school, but had the best grades in the class in another subject. Study the clues to discover which subject each child likes best and which they had the best grades in!

Nassim had the best grades in the subject Femi likes best, which isn't science or art.

Will had the best grades in history.

Jess likes music best.

Ross had the best grades in the subject Will likes best.

The child who likes science had the best grades in geography.

	Likes best	Had best grades
Femi		
Jess		
Nassim		
Ross		
Will		

The Amazing Maze

Jim is about to enter a maze. The walls of
the maze are very high, so Jim cannot see
over the top or climb them. The owner of
the maze tells Jim that everyone who has
entered the maze has needed assistance
to get back out again, because it is
so difficult!

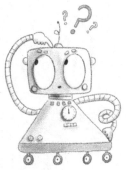

Here is a map of the maze. Jim has never
seen this map, he has never entered this maze before,
and he knows nobody who has been into it. He is sure he
can get to the middle of the maze (shown with a black
dot) and back out again without any help, because he
has a plan. What do you think Jim's plan might be?

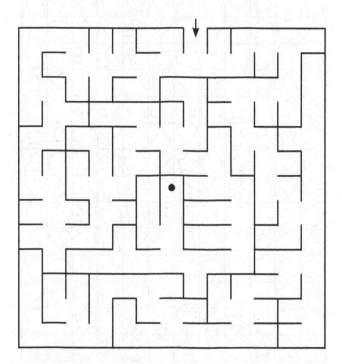

Six Symbols

Find this exact group of six squares in the larger grid:

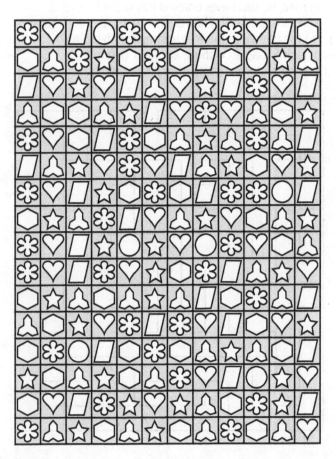

Painting by Numbers

You will need six different pencils or crayons for this puzzle: yellow, pink, orange, red, green, and blue.
To find out which to use in each pentagon, just follow the clues.

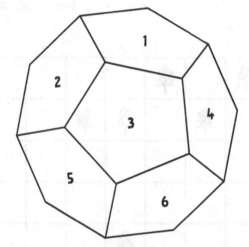

1 The red pentagon should not touch the yellow pentagon or the pink pentagon.

2 Pentagon 3 should not be orange.

3 Pentagon 6 should not be red.

4 Pentagon 1 should be pink.

5 The green pentagon should not touch the pink pentagon.

Camping in the Forest

Each tree has at least one tent in the next square across, up, or down from it. Tents do not touch each other's squares, not even diagonally. The numbers to the right of the grid show how many tents are in each horizontal row, and those below the grid show how many tents are in each vertical column. Draw triangles in the grid to show the position of each tent.

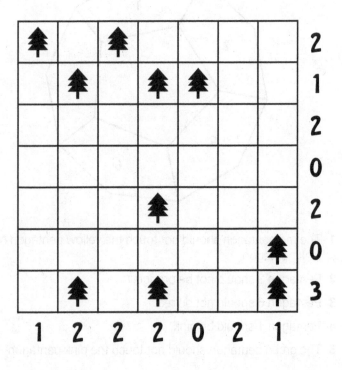

Star Sudoku

The numbers 1 to 9 must be placed
into the individual cells of each of the
six large triangles.

No digit appears more than once in
any horizontal row or diagonal line
of any length, even those rows and lines
interrupted by the central hexagon.
Some numbers are already in place.

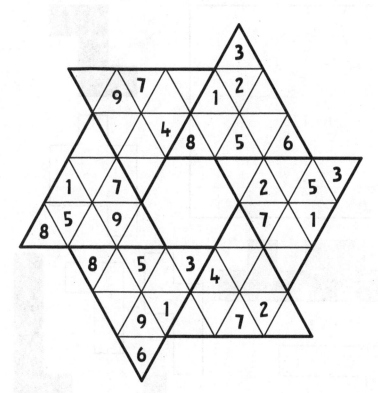

Square Shape

Can you fit all of these pieces into the square, so that it is completely filled, with no overhanging or overlapping shapes? No piece may be rotated or flipped over.

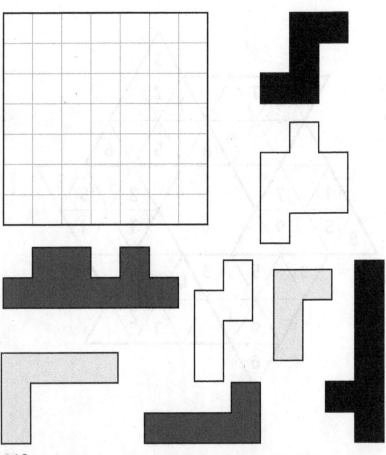

Bike Ride

The five children in this puzzle are about to set off on a bike ride. Each has a different bike and is a different age. See if you can figure out the details!

Adam is two years older than Leo, and Leo is two years older than the child who owns the orange bike.

The child who owns the blue bike is two years younger than Noah, whose bike is red.

Emma is younger than Isla, and Isla is one year younger than the child whose bike is green.

	9	10	11	12	13
Adam					
Emma					
Isla					
Leo					
Noah					

	Black	Blue	Green	Orange	Red
Adam					
Emma					
Isla					
Leo					
Noah					

Solutions

How many did you get right?
Check here for all of the answers!

Solutions!

Page 3

The letter A isn't opposite B or C
(cube 1), D or E (cube 3), so F.
The letter D isn't opposite C
(cube 2) or E (cube 3), so B.
So the letter E is opposite C.

Page 4

Page 5

The pairs are:
1 and 11
2 and 9
3 and 4
5 and 8
6 and 10
7 and 12

Page 6

1–D
2–C
3–A
4–E
5–B

Page 7

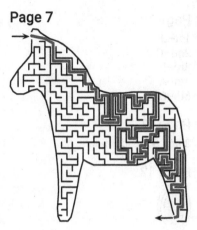

Page 8

Route C

Page 9

Solutions!

Page 10

1st–B
2nd–C
3rd–E
4th–A
5th–D

Page 11

3 and 8 are identical.

Page 12

Page 13

A heart: the sequence is heart, club, diamond, spade, repeated. A black arrow pointing up: the sequence of arrows is up, down, left, right.

Page 14

Yacht G is not in the second picture.

Page 15

Tower 2
It has 42 bricks (the others have 41 bricks).

Page 16

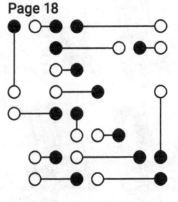

Page 17

From top to bottom:

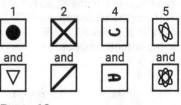

Page 18

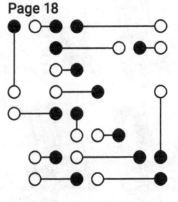

Page 19

Square C4 contains no symbol from column C.

Page 20

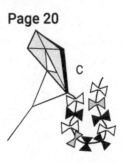

Page 21

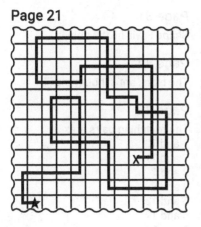

Page 25

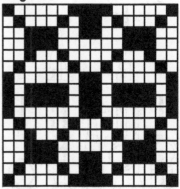

Page 22

C

It has an even number of white squares and an even number of black squares. All of the others have an odd number of white squares and an odd number of black squares.

Page 23

Wedge C was removed. Wedges are reflections of those directly opposite them.

Page 24

E

Page 26

Page 27

B

Solutions!

Page 28

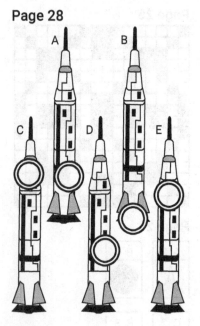

Page 29

F
A pairs with E.
B pairs with H.
C pairs with G.
D pairs with I.

Page 30

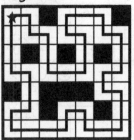

Page 31

Shape F will fill the hole.

Page 32

The black ant silhouette is 7.

Page 33

The matching pairs are:
1 and 10
2 and 11
3 and 7
4 and 8
5 and 13
6 and 12
9 and 14

Page 34

Page 35

A = 3
B = 5
C = 4
D = 1
E = 6
F = 2

Solutions!

Page 36

Page 37

The matching mugs are 2, 11, and 17.

Page 38

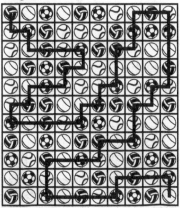

Page 39

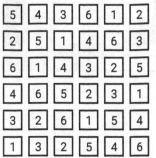

Page 40

1—Luke
2—Diane
3—Sanjay
4—Michelle
5—David

Page 41

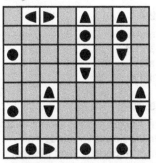

Page 42

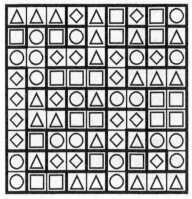

Solutions!

Page 43

	B	D	A	C
D	C	B		A
C		A	D	B
A	D	C	B	
B	A		C	D

Page 44

A, E, and L
B, C, and H
D, G, and I
F, J, and K

Page 45

Crown 1 belongs to Princess Pilar.
Crown 2 belongs to Prince Paul.
Crown 3 belongs to King Khaled.
Crown 4 belongs to Queen Cora.

Page 46

Jacket 6 has no exact match.
1 matches 10.
2 matches 8.
3 matches 9.
4 matches 12.
5 matches 11.
7 matches 13.

Page 47

There are 29 bubbles.
Mark blew 10.
Lucy blew 1.
Stella blew 4.
That gives a total of 26, so Mario blew 3.

Page 48

Remove the top three lines. There are now 7 small triangles and 2 large triangles (made up of 4 small triangles).

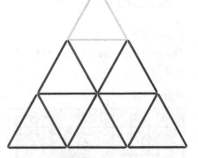

Page 49

Bucket C will fill.

Page 50

Page 51

Page 52

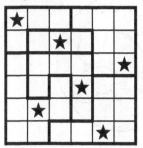

Page 53

X	O	O	O	X	X	O	O	X
O	X	O	X	O	X	X	X	O
X	O	O	O	X	X	X	O	O
X	O	X	X	X	O	X	O	O
X	O	O	O	X	O	O	X	X
O	X	X	O	O	X	O	O	O
X	O	O	X	X	O	O	X	X
O	O	X	X	O	X	X	O	X
X	X	O	X	X	X	O	O	X

Page 54

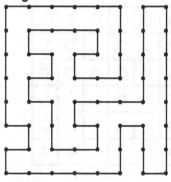

Page 55

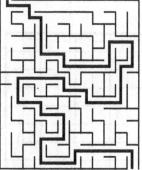

Page 56

Solutions!

Page 57

✻	☀	☾	☀	✻	☾
☀	✻	☀	☾	☀	☾
☾	✻	☀	✻	☀	✻
☾	☾	✻	☀	☾	☾
✻	☀	☾	✻	☀	☀
✻	☀	☾	☾	✻	✻

Page 58

Silhouette A matches the chimp.

Page 59

Page 60

Page 61

F cannot be paired. The pairs are:
A and K,
B and M,
C and O,
D and J,
E and L,
G and I,
H and N.

Page 62

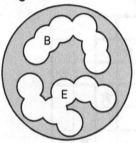

Page 63

Month	Child
January	Lola
February	Olivia
March	Jacob
April	Ethan
May	Oscar
June	Michael

120

Page 64

	1	2	3	4	5
Lucas				✓	
Amelia					✓
Jake	✓				
Ava			✓		
Oliver		✓			

Page 65

B contains the most building blocks.
A has 65.
B has 66.
C has 63.
D has 64.

Page 66

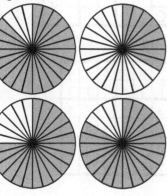

Page 67

Parts 1, 4, and 11 are not needed.

Page 68

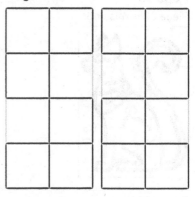

Page 69

Page 70

The identical arrows are 3 and 10.

Page 71

Page 72

View C matches the top down view.

Solutions!

Page 73

Piece C3 is missing:

Page 74

The correct code is:

Page 75

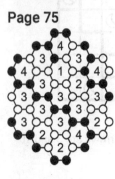

Page 76

Page 77

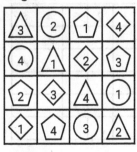

Page 78

						○	○
	○						
			○				○
○		○	○				○
					○		○
○							

Page 79

1	3	2	6	5	4
6	4	5	2	1	3
3	6	4	1	2	5
2	5	1	3	4	6
4	1	3	5	6	2
5	2	6	4	3	1

Page 80

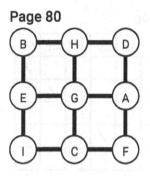

Page 81

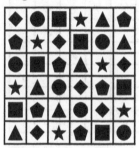

Page 82

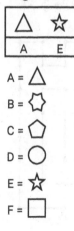

Page 83

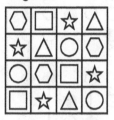

Page 84

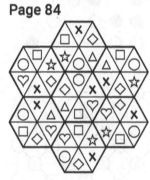

Page 85

D
From top to bottom, the number of sides of each shape increases by one, then decreases by two, then increases by one, then decreases by two, and this pattern of increases and decreases continues.

Page 86

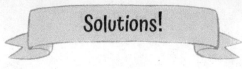
Page 87

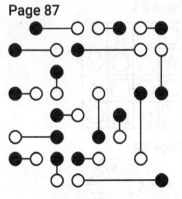

Page 88

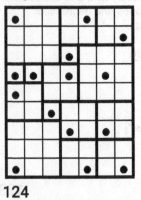

Page 89

Page 90

	1st	2nd	3rd	4th	5th
Emma					✓
Grace				✓	
Jay	✓				
Logan		✓			
Paulo			✓		

	6	7	8	9	10
Emma				✓	
Grace			✓		
Jay					✓
Logan		✓			
Paulo	✓				

Page 91

The correct code is 8 6 2 5.

Page 92

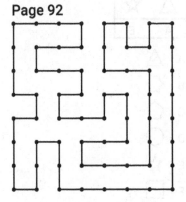

Solutions!

Page 93

Page 94

6	8	2	1	9	4	3	5	7
3	1	4	7	8	5	2	9	6
5	7	9	2	3	6	4	1	8
9	5	8	3	6	1	7	2	4
2	4	3	8	5	7	9	6	1
1	6	7	9	4	2	8	3	5
8	2	5	4	1	9	6	7	3
4	9	1	6	7	3	5	8	2
7	3	6	5	2	8	1	4	9

Page 95

Page 96

	China	Egypt	India	Peru
Maria	8	6	9	7
Leon	7	8	6	9
Omar	9	7	8	6
Sukie	6	9	7	8

Page 97

Page 98

	Turtle	Age
Tara	B	4
Terry	E	5
Thomas	C	6
Timmy	A	3
Tina	D	2

Page 99

Heaviest = △ Lightest = □
The heaviest shape isn't the
hexagon or circle (scale 1), or the
star or square (scale 3), so the
triangle is the heaviest shape.
The lightest shape isn't the star
(scale 1), or the circle (scale 2),
or the hexagon (scale 4), so the
square is the lightest shape.

125

Solutions!

Page 100

O	X	X	X	O	O	X	O	X
X	O	X	O	X	X	O	X	O
X	O	X	O	X	X	O	X	O
O	X	O	O	X	X	O	O	O
O	X	X	X	O	O	X	X	X
X	O	O	O	X	O	X	O	X
X	O	O	O	X	X	X	O	X
O	X	X	X	O	O	O	X	O
X	O	O	X	O	X	X	O	O

Page 101

The boxed marked "Hats" is on the top of the pile, and no box contains what it says on the label.

If you take a scarf from the top box, then the hats will be in the "Gloves" box, and the gloves will be in the "Scarves" box.

If you take a glove from the top box, then the hats will be in the "Scarves" box, and the scarves will be in the "Gloves" box.

Page 102

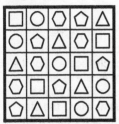

Page 103

Page 104

	Likes best	Had best grades
Femi	Geography	Music
Jess	Music	Science
Nassim	Science	Geography
Ross	History	Art
Will	Art	History

Page 105

On entering the maze, Jim puts his right hand on the right wall of the maze. As long as he keeps his right hand on the right wall, he will get to the middle and back out again.

It works just as well if Jim keeps his left hand on the left wall of the maze.

Solutions!

Page 106

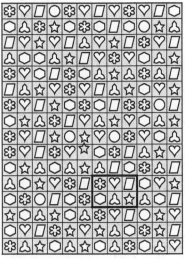

Page 107

1 = pink
2 = orange
3 = blue
4 = yellow
5 = red
6 = green

Pentagon 1 is pink (clue 4). It doesn't touch red (clue 1), and pentagon 6 isn't red (3), so pentagon 5 is red. Green doesn't touch pink (5), so pentagon 6 is green. Yellow doesn't touch red (1), so pentagon 4 is yellow. Pentagon 3 isn't orange (2), so blue (introduction). Pentagon 2 is orange.

Page 108

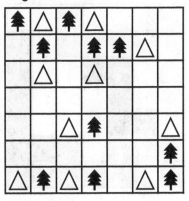

Page 109

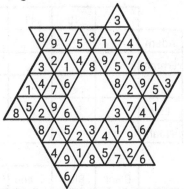

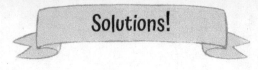

Solutions!

Page 110

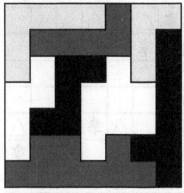

Page 111

	9	10	11	12	13
Adam					✓
Emma	✓				
Isla		✓			
Leo			✓		
Noah				✓	

	Black	Blue	Green	Orange	Red
Adam	✓				
Emma				✓	
Isla		✓			
Leo			✓		
Noah					✓